MY
DESTINY SCROLL

A Scribe's Record
Blank Journal

Journal design by

SHERI SCOTT

Artwork by
Karalyn Kohan
and
Janice Miller

MY DESTINY SCROLL: A Scribe's Record
Copyright ©2020 by Sheri Scott
Illustrations copyright ©2019 by Karalyn Kohan
Paintings copyright ©2019 by Janice Miller
Book design by Integrates Marketing
All rights reserved.

No part of this book may be used or reproduced in any manner whatsoever, or stored in a retrieval system, or transmitted in any form or by any means, electronic, mechanical, photocopying or otherwise, without written permission except in the case of brief quotations embodied in critical articles and reviews. For information address:

All Scripture English Standard Version

Published by: SHAREALIKE
An Imprint of SHARE *Publishing*
A division of Share Resources Inc.
Calgary, Alberta, Canada.
www.shareresourcesinc.com

ISBN 987-1-989269-34-3 (IngramSpark)
First Edition

MY DESTINY SCROLL

A Scribe's Record

journal: an account of day-to-day events

chronicle: a historical account of events arranged in order of time (usually without analysis or interpretation)

logbook: the full nautical record of a ship's voyage, the full record of a flight by an aircraft

diary: a record of experiences, ideas, or reflections kept regularly for private use

scribe: an official or public secretary or clerk, a copier of manuscripts. a member of a learned class in ancient times studying the Scriptures and serving as copyists, editors, teachers, and jurists.

record: a body of known or recorded facts about something or someone especially with reference to a particular sphere of activity that often forms a discernible pattern

For we are his workmanship, created in Christ Jesus for good works, which God prepared beforehand, that we should walk in them.

Ephesians 2:10

For you formed my inward parts; you knitted me together in my mother's womb. I praise you, for I am fearfully and wonderfully made. Wonderful are your works; my soul knows it very well. My frame was not hidden from you, when I was being made in secret, intricately woven in the depths of the earth. Your eyes saw my unformed substance; in your book were written, every one of them, the days that were formed for me, when as yet there was none of them.

Psalm 139:13-16 ESV

In him we have obtained an inheritance, having been predestined according to the purpose of him who works all things according to the counsel of his will.

Ephesians 1:11 ESV

But when he who had set me apart before I was born, and who called me by his grace.

Galatians 1:15 ESV

Even as he chose us in him before the foundation of the world, that we should be holy and blameless before him. In love, he predestined us for adoption as sons through Jesus Christ, according to the purpose of his will.

Galatians 1:15 ESV

Jesus said to him, "I am the way, and the truth, and the life. No one comes to the Father except through me.

John 14:6 ESV

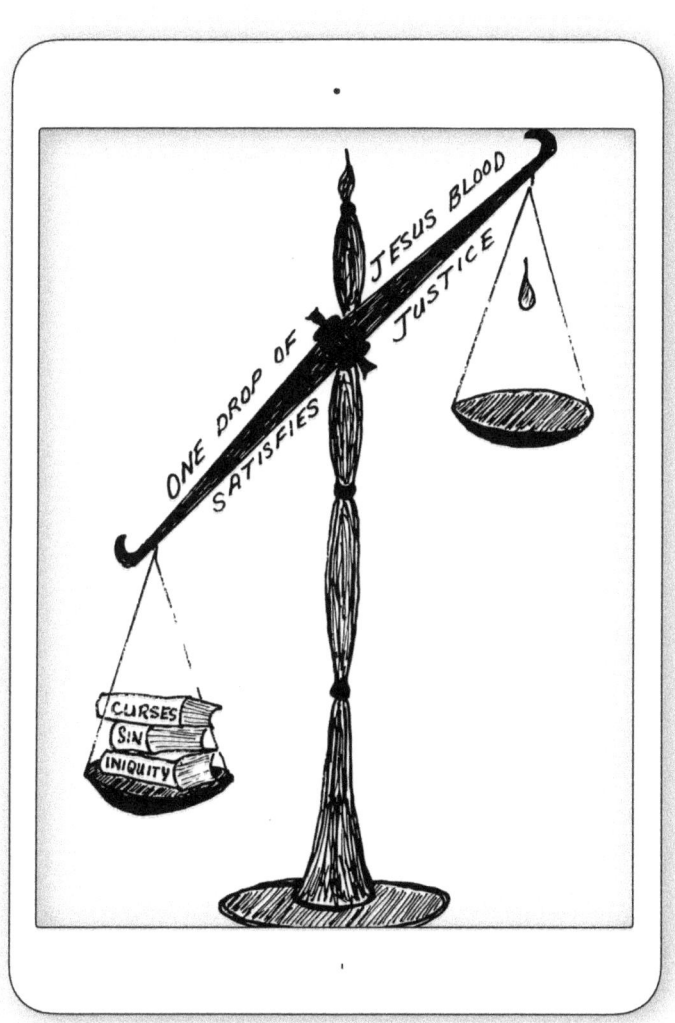

These all died in faith, not having received the things promised, but having seen them and greeted them from afar, and having acknowledged that they were strangers and exiles on the earth.

Hebrews 11:13 ESV

Therefore, brothers, be all the more diligent to make your calling and election sure, for if you practice these qualities you will never fall. For in this way there will be richly provided for you an entrance into the eternal kingdom of our Lord and Savior Jesus Christ.

2 Peter 1:10-11 ESV

And those whom he predestined he also called, and those whom he called he also justified, and those whom he justified he also glorified.

Romans 8:30 ESV

But I do not account my life of any value nor as precious to myself, if only I may finish my course and the ministry that I received from the Lord Jesus, to testify to the gospel of the grace of God.

Acts 20:24 ESV

For he will complete what he appoints for me, and many such things are in his mind.

Job 23:14 ESV

And I saw the dead, great and small, standing before the throne, and books were opened. Then another book was opened, which is the book of life. And the dead were judged by what was written in the books, according to what they had done.

Revelation 20:12 ESV

*The End
from the beginning*

www.ingramcontent.com/pod-product-compliance
Lightning Source LLC
Chambersburg PA
CBHW061210070526
44583CB00025B/3194